A Learn To Read book:

THE
FOOTBALL
MATCH

ADRIAN LOBLEY

Books by Adrian Lobley

Learning Maths
The Football Maths Book (Ages 4-7)
The Football Maths Book - The Re-match! (Ages 5-8)
The Football Maths Book - The Christmas Match (Ages 6-8)
The Football Maths Book - The Birthday Party (Ages 7-8)
The Football Maths Book - The World Cup (Age 9-10)

Learning to Read
A Learn to Read Book: The Football Match (Ages 4-5)
A Learn to Read Book: The Tennis Match (Ages 4-5)

Historical Fiction
Kane and the Mystery of the Missing World Cup (Ages 7-10)
Kane and the Christmas Football Adventure (Ages 7-10)

Humour
The Ridiculous Adventures of Sidebottom and McPlop (Ages 7-10)

For more info go to: www.adrianlobley.com

With thanks to:
Anne Lobley, Sam Pierre, Malcolm Lobley, Sebastian Wraith-Lobley, Emma Turner,
Beverley Harris, Sarah Wraith, Pat Martin, Anthony Backhouse, Sabrine Watmough, Logan Baxendale

and
the teachers and pupils of
Athelstan Community Primary School,
Sherburn, N.Yorks

All illustrations by:
Ella Loren Bulatao

To Sebastian.

1. Explain that the aim of this adventure book is for the child to make choices as she/he moves through it, to try and arrive at one of the GOAL pages. Help the child read the word GOAL now.

2. Every time the child scores a goal by arriving at a GOAL page, then he/she should turn to the Scores page at the rear of the book and update the match score on a new row.

3. Where blank underlines appear _____ through the book, the child should write in her/his name (pencil is recommended).

As a parent I have found that segmenting certain words works well eg 'p-a-s-t'. Saying each letter phonetically (so 's' is pronounced 'sss') then produces the sound of the word.

I also learnt that sitting the child at a table in a quiet place is effective, as is emphasising the fun element of the book.

Illustrations in the book do not relate to the words next to them. This is so the child reads what is written, rather than using pictures to memorise or guess words.

Go to page

Kick off 3

2

Go to page

Kick it ➡ 5

or

Blast it ➡ 7

4

GOAL

Turn to the Scores section at the back of the book and update the score,
then go to page 9

GOAL

Turn to the Scores section at the back of the book and update the score,
then go to page 9

8

Go to page

Kick off   11

Go to page

Boot it 13

or

Blast it _____ 15

Write your name here, then make your page choice

Writing aid:

a	b	c	d	e	f	g	h	i	j	k	l	m
n	o	p	q	r	s	t	u	v	w	x	y	z

Turn to the Scores section at the back of the book and update the score, then go to page 17

MISS

Go to page 19

16

18

Go to page

Run back ⇨ 25

or

Tackle a man ⇨ 21

20

Go to page

Dribble ⇨ 27

or

Cross it _____ ⇨ 29

Writing aid:

a	b	c	d	e	f	g	h	i	j	k	l	m
n	o	p	q	r	s	t	u	v	w	x	y	z

Go to page

_____ runs fast 31

or

Go past a man 33

Writing aid:

a	b	c	d	e	f	g	h	i	j	k	l	m
n	o	p	q	r	s	t	u	v	w	x	y	z

24

<u>Go to page</u>

_____ trips a man  35

or

Fall in the box  37

Writing aid:

a	b	c	d	e	f	g	h	i	j	k	l	m
n	o	p	q	r	s	t	u	v	w	x	y	z

Go to page

Win penalty. Kick it left ⟹ 39

or

Win penalty. Kick it hard ⟹ 41

Go to page

A shot on target ⇨ 41

or

A header at goal ⇨ 39

34

Go to page

Say sorry ➡ 19

or

Ref pulls out a card ➡ 43

Go to page

Yell at the ref  43

or

_____ wins a penalty  39

Writing aid:

a	b	c	d	e	f	g	h	i	j	k	l	m
n	o	p	q	r	s	t	u	v	w	x	y	z

38

Turn to the Scores section at the back of the book and update the score,
then go to page 17

MISS

Go to page 19

Red card. End of match

Time is up. End of match

Scores

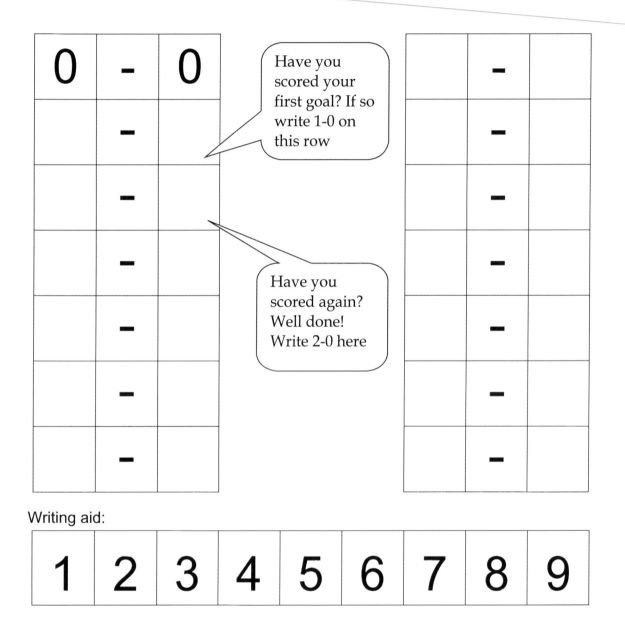

Writing aid:

Books by Adrian Lobley

Maths

Book 1: The Football Maths Book   (Age 4-7)

The Soccer Math Book (US version)

El libro de matemáticas de fútbol (Spanish version)

Book 2: The Football Maths Book   The Re-match! (Age 5-8)

Book 3: The Football Maths Book   The Christmas Match (Age 6-8)

Book 4: The Football Maths Book   The Birthday Party (Age 7-8)

Book 5: The Football Maths Book   The World Cup (Age 9-10)

Reading

A Learn to Read Book: The Football Match (Ages 4-5)
A Learn to Read Book: The Tennis Match   (Ages 4-5)

Historical Fiction

Kane and the Mystery of the Missing World Cup
Kane and the Christmas Football Adventure

Humour

The Ridiculous Adventures of Sidebottom and McPlop (Ages 7-10)

For more information go to www.adrianlobley.com

Printed in Great Britain
by Amazon